Z-SAT

Zombie Survival Aptitude Test

Z-SAT

ZOMBIE SURVIVAL APTITUDE TEST

Written and Illustrated by
CASEY B. BASSETT

Published by Lulu Enterprises, Inc
www.lulu.com

Printed in the United States of America

Library of Congress Cataloging-in-Publication Date
Bassett, Casey B.
Z-sat : zombie survival aptitude test / Casey B. Bassett.

ISBN 978-0-557-89084-2

First Edition

*Special thanks for the
support from my friends, family,
and fellow zombie survivalists.
When the dead rise,
meet me at the depot.*

...and don't forget to bring this book.

Z-SAT

Zombie Survival Aptitude Test

NOTICE: THE FOLLOWING INFORMATION MUST BE READ IN ORDER TO COMPLETE THIS TEST EFFECTIVELY.

There are different types of zombies that have different characteristics. They can either be fast or slow, see below for definition. The manner in killing can also vary; zombies can be killed by either a head kill only (HK) or a head and/or body kill (HBK).

ZOMBIE CHARACTERISTICS:

SPEEDS:
Slow/Fast

Slow: The limited ability to move in a manner that only one foot is located on the ground at all times when in travel or pursuit -- I.e. walking at a moderate or less than moderate speed.

Fast: The advanced ability to move more rapidly, in which for an instant both feet are off the ground when in travel or pursuit. -- I.e. running and/or sprinting.

KILLING METHODS:
Head Kill (HK)/Head and/or Body Kill (HBK)

Head Kill (HK): Removing the head or destroying the brain is the only means of killing or death.

Head and/or Body Kill (HBK): Removing the head or destroying the brain and/or destroying the body are the optimum means of killing or death.

DEFINING EACH ZOMBIE TYPE:
Slow/HK, Slow/HBK, Fast/HK, Fast/HBK

1. **Slow/HK:** STANDARD – A zombie that can only walk and can only be killed by removing the head or destroying the brain.

2. **Slow/HBK:** A zombie that can only walk and be killed by removing the head or destroying the brain and/or destroying the body.

3. **Fast/HK:** A zombie that has the ability to run and can only be killed by removing the head or destroying the brain.

4. **Fast/HBK:** A zombie that has the ability to run and can be killed by removing the head or destroying the brain and/or destroying the body.

> **NOTICE:** For the purpose of this test, all the following questions will be based on, the standard: **Zombie Type: Slow/HK.**

INFECTION:

For the purpose of this test, the zombie infection is virus based. The zombie virus can only be spread or transferred to its victim by blood or saliva. It is not airborne and cannot be made airborne.

Example: Incineration of the virus or zombie will not spread the virus via vapors, smoke, or any other types of discharge created from incineration.

QUESTION TYPES:

1. **Fact Based Multiple Choice:** These types of questions are based on general facts and knowledge. Answering these questions correctly is important, because using deductive reasoning in a given situation can mean the difference between life and death.

2. **Situational Multiple Choice:** These types of questions test your ability to respond appropriately in a given situation.

3. **Situational Illustration Multiple Choice:** These types of questions test your ability to look at a collection of different objects or situations and determining the best choice.

4. **True and False:** These types of questions determine your ability to identify one incorrect answer from one correct answer.

5. **Personal Evaluation:** This section of the test evaluates your physical attributes and assigns a percentage according to your strengths and weaknesses.

The purposes of type **1**, **2**, **3** and **4** are all for testing your mental and reasoning abilities.

The purpose of type **5** is to evaluate your physical attributes and characteristics.

<u>IMPORTANT!</u>

<u>REMEMBER:</u> ONLY USE A NO. 2 PENCIL TO COMPLETE THIS TEST.

When you see the **STOP SIGN** in the bottom right hand corner of the page, you have completed the *Z-SAT Reasoning Test*. Please remember to review your answers and complete any questions you might have missed.

After your review use the scoring guide in the back of the book to grade your answers. This will determine your chances of surviving a zombie outbreak.

<u>**DO NOT CHANGE ANSWERS ONCE YOU GO PAST THE STOP SIGN!**</u>

**THIS IS THE BEGINNING OF THE
ZOMBIE SURVIVAL APTITUDE TEST**

1. What is a zombie?

   Ⓐ A person under a spell or hypnotized
   Ⓑ A dead person
   Ⓒ A reanimated corpse
   Ⓓ A drunken homeless guy

2. Zombies are not living.

   Ⓐ True
   Ⓑ False

3. Zombies are intelligent.

   Ⓐ True
   Ⓑ False

4. What special ability do zombies have?

   Ⓐ Never tire
   Ⓑ Super speed
   Ⓒ Super strength
   Ⓓ None

5. All zombies can run.

   Ⓐ True
   Ⓑ False

6. Zombies only desire is to feed.

   Ⓐ True
   Ⓑ False

7. All zombies fear fire.

   Ⓐ True
   Ⓑ False

8. What do zombies primarily need?

   (A) To kill humans
   (B) Feed on human flesh
   (C) Feed on human brains
   (D) Both B and C

9. Zombies cannot survive under water.

   (A) True
   (B) False

10. Do not be afraid of zombies. They are more scared of you than you are of them.

    (A) True
    (B) False

11. Which of the following zombies is considered to be the most dangerous?

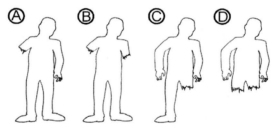

    (A) Letter A
    (B) Letter B
    (C) Letter C
    (D) Letter D

12. What do zombies fear?

    (A) Fire
    (B) Garlic
    (C) Silver
    (D) Nothing

13. Zombies can swim.

    Ⓐ True
    Ⓑ False

14. Zombies are not strong enough to break through a standard household window.

    Ⓐ True
    Ⓑ False

15. Which of the following zombies is considered to be the second most dangerous?

    Ⓐ Letter A
    Ⓑ Letter B
    Ⓒ Letter C
    Ⓓ Letter D

16. Zombies feel mercy.

    Ⓐ True
    Ⓑ False

17. Zombies cannot break through the glass on a vehicle.

    Ⓐ True
    Ⓑ False

18. Zombies can communicate with people.

    Ⓐ True
    Ⓑ False

19. We can communicate with zombies, and sometimes even convince them not to harm us.

    Ⓐ True
    Ⓑ False

20. Which of the following zombies is considered to be the third most dangerous?

    Ⓐ Letter A
    Ⓑ Letter B
    Ⓒ Letter C
    Ⓓ Letter D

21. Zombies can operate firearms.

    Ⓐ True
    Ⓑ False

22. Zombies cannot drown.

    Ⓐ True
    Ⓑ False

23. Zombies cannot see you if you do not move.

    Ⓐ True
    Ⓑ False

24. Zombies can communicate with each other.

    Ⓐ True
    Ⓑ False

25. Which of the following zombies is considered to be the least dangerous?

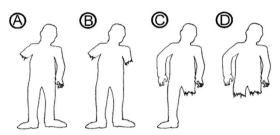

Ⓐ Letter A
Ⓑ Letter B
Ⓒ Letter C
Ⓓ Letter D

26. Zombies have "super senses" (vision, hearing, smell, etc.).

Ⓐ True
Ⓑ False

27. All zombies are physically weak.

Ⓐ True
Ⓑ False

28. Not all zombies want to inflict harm on you.

Ⓐ True
Ⓑ False

29. Zombies can freeze to death.

Ⓐ True
Ⓑ False

30. Which type of zombie is capable of feeling pain and emotions?

   Ⓐ Voodoo zombies
   Ⓑ Recently reanimated zombies
   Ⓒ All types of zombies
   Ⓓ None

31. Everything you have seen in "zombie movies" is considered true.

   Ⓐ True
   Ⓑ False

32. What is the most popular name for a complete zombie takeover?

   Ⓐ Z-Day
   Ⓑ Zombie Armageddon
   Ⓒ Zombie Apocalypse
   Ⓓ Zombie Dooms Day

33. If bitten by a zombie, you can be cured.

   Ⓐ True
   Ⓑ False

34. What happens if you are bitten by a zombie?

   Ⓐ Sickness
   Ⓑ Death
   Ⓒ Reanimation
   Ⓓ All of the above

35. Zombie outbreaks do not spread very fast.

   Ⓐ True
   Ⓑ False

36. A zombie bite will not kill you if the wound is treated as soon as possible.

    Ⓐ True
    Ⓑ False

37. Only large bites or wounds from a zombie will kill you.

    Ⓐ True
    Ⓑ False

38. What is the cure or treatment if infected by a zombie?

    Ⓐ Bullet to the head
    Ⓑ Amputate bitten limb
    Ⓒ Neosporin and/or balm
    Ⓓ None

39. A zombie's flesh is edible and safe for consumption when cooked properly.

    Ⓐ True
    Ⓑ False

40. A zombie can still infect a person after it dies.

    Ⓐ True
    Ⓑ False

41. After killing a zombie, just leave it; do not bother disposing of its corpse.

    Ⓐ True
    Ⓑ False

42. Where do you shoot a zombie in order to kill it?

   Ⓐ Letter A
   Ⓑ Letter B
   Ⓒ Letter C
   Ⓓ Letter D

43. You can kill a zombie by shooting it in the heart.

   Ⓐ True
   Ⓑ False

44. The best method of killing a zombie is to remove the zombies head and/or destroy its brain.

   Ⓐ True
   Ⓑ False

45. What is the best way to kill a zombie?

   Ⓐ Breaking its neck
   Ⓑ Shoot/destroy/remove the heart
   Ⓒ Shooting it in the head
   Ⓓ Removing its head or destroying its brain

46. Military experience will greatly improve your chance of survival.

   Ⓐ True
   Ⓑ False

47. Completely severing the head will immobilize any zombie.

   Ⓐ True
   Ⓑ False

48. When attempting to kill a zombie with a crowbar, which of the following areas on the head should you aim for?

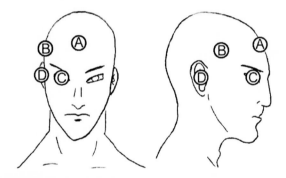

   Ⓐ Letter A
   Ⓑ Letter B
   Ⓒ Letter C
   Ⓓ Letter D

49. Hand-to-hand combat is the worst form of combat.

   Ⓐ True
   Ⓑ False

50. *Situation:* A teammate arrives back at camp with fresh wounds. He insists that they were from an accidental fall. What action should you take?

   Ⓐ Believe him; we are all on the same side
   Ⓑ Watch him closely to see if he starts to get sick

Ⓒ Shoot him; there is no reason to take any chances
Ⓓ Tie him down and simply explain your concerns and
   need for precautions

51. When in combat, the closer to the zombies the better.

Ⓐ True
Ⓑ False

52. Long range combat is strongly discouraged.

Ⓐ True
Ⓑ False

53. Being skilled in martial arts is a great advantage when combating zombies.

Ⓐ True
Ⓑ False

54. Which of the following areas should you shoot a zombie in order to only drop it and/or slow it down without killing it?

Ⓐ Letter A
Ⓑ Letter B
Ⓒ Letter C
Ⓓ Letter D

55. Combat with zombies should always be a last resort.

    Ⓐ True
    Ⓑ False

56. Which type of combat should always be avoided?

    Ⓐ Hand-to-hand
    Ⓑ Point blank
    Ⓒ Closed quarters
    Ⓓ Long range

57. The odds are in your favor over the zombies when in combat.

    Ⓐ True
    Ⓑ False

58. Military combat experience is not useful when combating zombies.

    Ⓐ True
    Ⓑ False

59. Which of the following area on the human skull is the strongest?

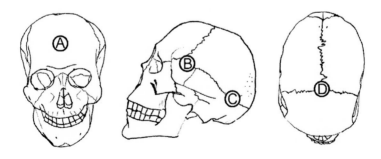

- Ⓐ Letter A
- Ⓑ Letter B
- Ⓒ Letter C
- Ⓓ Letter D

60. Which of the following is not a good camouflage technique?

- Ⓐ Avoiding unnecessary movement
- Ⓑ Using textures
- Ⓒ Staying in the shadows
- Ⓓ Using contrasts

61. What position is the best and most practical when firing a gun?

- Ⓐ Prone position
- Ⓑ Sitting position
- Ⓒ Standing position (point shooting)
- Ⓓ Kneeling position

62. Which of the following areas on the human skull is the weakest?

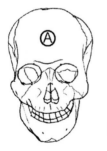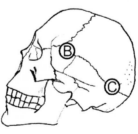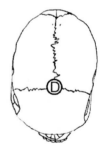

- Ⓐ Letter A
- Ⓑ Letter B
- Ⓒ Letter C
- Ⓓ Letter D

63. Hunting experience will not be helpful in a zombie outbreak.

    Ⓐ True
    Ⓑ False

64. When you are in a hand-to-hand combat situation, and are holding your primary weapon in your hand. Which of the following areas on the zombie should you grab with your free hand?

    Ⓐ Hair
    Ⓑ Neck/Throat
    Ⓒ Chest
    Ⓓ Arm/Wrist

65. An aluminum baseball bat is better than a wooden baseball bat.

    Ⓐ True
    Ⓑ False

66. Which of the following is the best weapon to carry in a zombie survival situation?

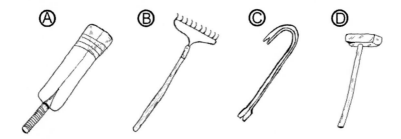

- Ⓐ Letter A
- Ⓑ Letter B
- Ⓒ Letter C
- Ⓓ Letter D

67. Firearms are the best weapons to kill a zombie in any situation.

- Ⓐ True
- Ⓑ False

68. *Situation:* A person on your team that you hate is trapped by zombies. You have the means to stop them. What action should you take?

- Ⓐ Let the zombie kill the person and say there was nothing you could do
- Ⓑ Throw the teammate a weapon and just walk away from the situation
- Ⓒ Let the zombie kill the person because it would be better for the team
- Ⓓ Kill the zombie and rescue the teammate

69. Which of the following is the best weapon to carry in a zombie survival situation?

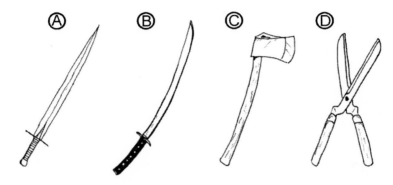

Ⓐ Letter A
Ⓑ Letter B
Ⓒ Letter C
Ⓓ Letter D

70. A chainsaw is better than a sword.

Ⓐ True
Ⓑ False

71. What would be the greatest benefit of using a crowbar as your choice of weapon?

Ⓐ Versatile
Ⓑ Durable
Ⓒ Lightweight
Ⓓ All of the above

72. Friendly fire is not something to be concerned with.

Ⓐ True
Ⓑ False

73. Which of the following weapons is the most reliable?

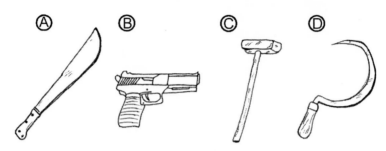

Ⓐ Letter A
Ⓑ Letter B
Ⓒ Letter C
Ⓓ Letter D

74. Which of the following household items is the best weapon?

Ⓐ Sledgehammer
Ⓑ Claw hammer
Ⓒ Crowbar
Ⓓ Baseball bat

75. What is the greatest disadvantage when using the claw hammer as a weapon?

Ⓐ Limited reach
Ⓑ Not heavy enough for a one hit kill
Ⓒ Some wooden handles might brake on impact
Ⓓ The claw could potentially get fixed in the victim's skull

76. *Situation:* You are deep in infected territory, zombies are everywhere. Which weapon do you choose to escape quickly and undetected?

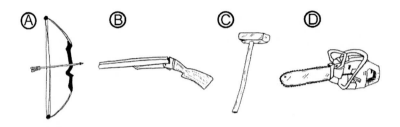

Ⓐ Letter A
Ⓑ Letter B
Ⓒ Letter C
Ⓓ Letter D

77. Firearms should always be your first choice when killing a zombie.

Ⓐ True
Ⓑ False

78. *Situation:* You are deep in an infected territory. Zombies are everywhere, which weapon do you choose to escape quickly and undetected?

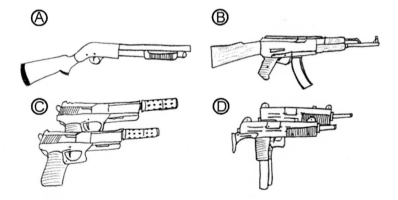

Ⓐ Letter A
Ⓑ Letter B
Ⓒ Letter C
Ⓓ Letter D

79. A pitch fork will not kill a zombie.

   Ⓐ True
   Ⓑ False

80. A sling blade is a light-weight and compact weapon of choice.

   Ⓐ True
   Ⓑ False

81. *Situation:* You and your group are camping overnight in the woods in unfamiliar territory. A single zombie wanders into your camp. Which weapon do you use to kill it?

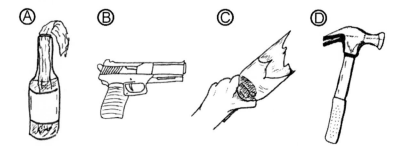

   Ⓐ Letter A
   Ⓑ Letter B
   Ⓒ Letter C
   Ⓓ Letter D

82. What is the greatest advantage of an edged weapon over a gun?

   Ⓐ Does not need reloaded
   Ⓑ Even if it is dull, it will still kill a zombie
   Ⓒ Will never break
   Ⓓ All of the above

83. Over the period of a month, which of the following do you choose as your primary weapon?

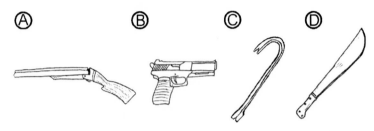

Ⓐ   Ⓑ   Ⓒ   Ⓓ

    Ⓐ Letter A
    Ⓑ Letter B
    Ⓒ Letter C
    Ⓓ Letter D

84. A fencing sword is the best sword to kill a zombie.

    Ⓐ True
    Ⓑ False

85. What is the greatest advantage of the machete?

    Ⓐ Lightweight, versatile, and durable
    Ⓑ Easy to conceal and never dulls
    Ⓒ Common to find and easy use
    Ⓓ Both A and C

86. *Situation:* A zombie is attempting to attack you, and your gun has no more ammo. You have a small knife with you, but you have never used it. You are unsure of its capabilities. What action should you take?

    Ⓐ Take a chance and try to kill the zombie with the knife
    Ⓑ Do not risk it, try to escape without confrontation
    Ⓒ Try to kill the zombie without the knife
    Ⓓ Wrestle the zombie down to the ground then run away

87. What is the best weapon for hand-to-hand combat?

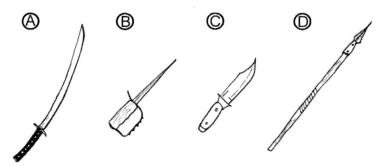

   Ⓐ   Ⓑ   Ⓒ   Ⓓ

Ⓐ Letter A
Ⓑ Letter B
Ⓒ Letter C
Ⓓ Letter D

88. A spade is a better weapon than a crowbar.

Ⓐ True
Ⓑ False

89. What is the advantage of a blunt weapon over an edged weapon?

Ⓐ Less chance of cutting yourself or others
Ⓑ Less blood splatter
Ⓒ They do not need sharpening
Ⓓ Both A and C

90. Which of the following is the best edged weapon of choice?

Ⓐ Ax
Ⓑ Single-handed hatchet
Ⓒ Single-handed sword
Ⓓ Japanese Samurai Katana

91. *Situation:* You are taking refuge in your house when the zombie outbreak occurs. You realize that you do not own any firearms or large bladed weapons. What action do you take?

   Ⓐ Travel to the nearest gun store and get some weapons
   Ⓑ Use whatever you have at your disposal in your house
   Ⓒ You do not need a weapon because you are in your house
   Ⓓ Loot your next door neighbors for a good weapon

92. What is the greatest risk when using a Japanese Samurai Katana?

   Ⓐ Too sharp, chance of hurting yourself
   Ⓑ Not sharp enough to cut through a zombie's skull
   Ⓒ Katanas dull too easily
   Ⓓ Most Katanas sold are not durable enough to kill multiple zombies

93. Which of the following angles is best when sharpening a blade on a sharpening stone?

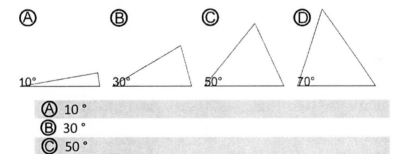

   Ⓐ 10 °
   Ⓑ 30 °
   Ⓒ 50 °
   Ⓓ 70 °

94. Which of the following is silent and accurate?

   Ⓐ Chinese throwing stars
   Ⓑ Compound bow and arrow
   Ⓒ Shotgun
   Ⓓ Silenced pistol

95. Which of the following firearms holds the most cartridges?

    (A) Mossberg 500
    (B) Mac-10
    (C) Beretta 92F
    (D) Remington 700

96. Which gauge of cartridge will cause the most amount of damage to a zombie?

    (A) .45 ACP
    (B) 12 Gauge
    (C) .410 Bore
    (D) 20 Gauge

97. Which of the following cartridges is the smallest?

    (A) .50 BMG
    (B) .308 Winchester
    (C) .22 LR
    (D) .300 Win Mag

98. Which of the following cartridges is the largest?

    (A) .50 BMG
    (B) .308 Winchester
    (C) .22 LR
    (D) .300 Win Mag

99. Which cartridge has the most stopping power?

    (A) 9mm
    (B) .45
    (C) .357
    (D) .22

100. What are the worst conditions for ammunition?

     Ⓐ Cold
     Ⓑ Heat
     Ⓒ Moisture
     Ⓓ Both B and C

101. You should always keep gun powder _____?

     Ⓐ At room temperature
     Ⓑ Cool and dry
     Ⓒ Warm and/or in direct sunlight
     Ⓓ None of the above

102. If you choose a rifle with a stainless steel barrel, it will_____?

     Ⓐ Stay cooler when firing and will result in longer life
     Ⓑ Retain heat longer making it somewhat more prone to damage compared to other types of barrels
     Ⓒ Rust when it comes in contact with water
     Ⓓ Have less recoil

103. Choose the best weapon to kill a zombie.

     Ⓐ Assault rifle
     Ⓑ Shotgun
     Ⓒ .22 Rifle
     Ⓓ Depends on the shooter

104. Rust can ruin a firearm. The best type of metal to prevent your firearm from rusting is_____.

     Ⓐ Stainless steel
     Ⓑ Chrome
     Ⓒ Nickel
     Ⓓ All the above

105. If not properly oiled and/or maintained, stainless steel firearms will_____.

   Ⓐ Rust
   Ⓑ Corrode
   Ⓒ Tarnish
   Ⓓ Not be affect

106. Oiling is not necessary for all firearms finished in_____.

   Ⓐ Paint
   Ⓑ Teflon
   Ⓒ Chrome nickel
   Ⓓ All of the above

107. *Situation:* You and your team are traveling through the woods when you are suddenly faced with a horde of zombies. Your team runs ahead of you to kill them. Which of the following weapons is best for you to use?

   Ⓐ Machete
   Ⓑ Shotgun
   Ⓒ Assault Rifle
   Ⓓ Crowbar

108. *Situation:* You and your team are traveling through the woods when you are suddenly faced with a horde of zombies. Your team runs ahead of you to kill them. Which of the following weapons is the worst for you to use?

Ⓐ Machete
Ⓑ Shotgun
Ⓒ Assault Rifle
Ⓓ Crowbar

109. If you are shooting at a zombie that is moving parallel to you at less than 230 meters, where should you aim your firearm on the target?

Ⓐ Directly in the middle
Ⓑ One body length ahead of it
Ⓒ On the front edge of it
Ⓓ 2.3 meters in front of it

110. If you are shooting at a zombie that is moving parallel to you at more than 230 meters, where should you aim your firearm on the target?

Ⓐ One body length
Ⓑ Two body lengths
Ⓒ Three body lengths
Ⓓ None of the above

111. When using a loaded firearm, what is the most important thing you should always remember?

Ⓐ Keep the firearm aimed at the ground at all times
Ⓑ Keep the safety on at all times, even if there are zombies in the area
Ⓒ Keep the firearm aimed at eye level at all times
Ⓓ Keep your finger off the trigger, and on the trigger guard, until you are ready to shoot

112. Failure to keep your finger on the trigger guard and having an accidental discharge could result in what?

Ⓐ Killing or wounding yourself or a teammate
Ⓑ Alerting nearby zombies
Ⓒ Alerting nearby survivors
Ⓓ All of the above

113. When shooting a zombie in the head, statistically, which shot will be the best and most likely to hit the target?

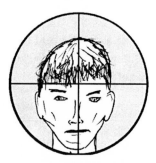

Ⓐ First shot
Ⓑ Second shot
Ⓒ Depends on the shooter
Ⓓ Unpredictable/random

114. When ambushing a group of zombies, or other survivors, what are the best weapons to use?

   Ⓐ Firearms
   Ⓑ Bare hands
   Ⓒ Basic weapons (crowbars, machetes, hammers, etc.)
   Ⓓ It depends on the people in the group and where the ambush is taking place

115. What is the maximum distance that fragmentation grenades can cause injury?

   Ⓐ 5-10 meters
   Ⓑ 20 meters
   Ⓒ 50 meters
   Ⓓ 70-100 meters

116. On average, what is the time delay on grenades?

   Ⓐ 0-1 second
   Ⓑ 3-5 seconds
   Ⓒ 8-10 seconds
   Ⓓ 13-15 seconds

117. Which of the following cartridges is a .357 Magnum?

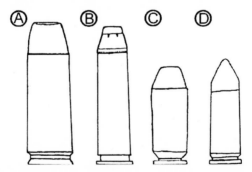

   Ⓐ Letter A
   Ⓑ Letter B
   Ⓒ Letter C
   Ⓓ Letter D

118. What is the maximum distance from a grenade that zombies will consistently be killed/disabled?

    Ⓐ Within 2 meters of the blast area
    Ⓑ Within 5 meters of the blast area
    Ⓒ Within 10 meters of the blast area
    Ⓓ Within 15 meters of the blast area

119. Which of the following cartridges is a .50 Action Express?

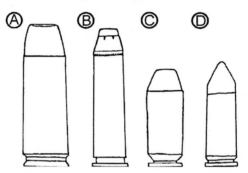

    Ⓐ Letter A
    Ⓑ Letter B
    Ⓒ Letter C
    Ⓓ Letter D

120. When fighting long range, within what distance will wind deflection not affect the bullets trajectory?

    Ⓐ Within 90 meters
    Ⓑ Within 180 meters
    Ⓒ Within 275 meters
    Ⓓ Within 365 meters

121. Which of the following grenades is most likely to kill a zombie?

    Ⓐ Smoke
    Ⓑ Incendiary
    Ⓒ Chemical
    Ⓓ Fragmentation

122. Which of the following cartridges is a 9x19mm Parabellum?

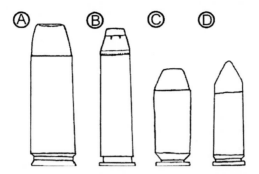

Ⓐ Letter A
Ⓑ Letter B
Ⓒ Letter C
Ⓓ Letter D

123. Tear gas is very effective against zombies.

Ⓐ True
Ⓑ False

124. Which of the following cartridges is a .40 S&W?

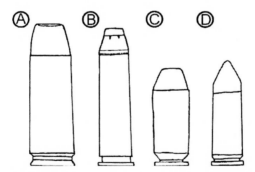

Ⓐ Letter A
Ⓑ Letter B
Ⓒ Letter C
Ⓓ Letter D

125. What is the maximum distance that shotguns are effective when using buckshot rather than slugs?

    Ⓐ 18 meters
    Ⓑ 35 meters
    Ⓒ 90 meters
    Ⓓ 90+ meters

126. Using chain mail for armor will guarantee your safety.

    Ⓐ True
    Ⓑ False

127. It is better to wear armor that will slow you down than not to wear armor and be fast.

    Ⓐ True
    Ⓑ False

128. The advantages of body armors outweigh its disadvantages.

    Ⓐ True
    Ⓑ False

129. Armoring your vehicle is better than armoring yourself.

    Ⓐ True
    Ⓑ False

130. Hiding in a car is good protection in a zombie attack.

    Ⓐ True
    Ⓑ False

131. Chainmail is unbreakable.

    Ⓐ True
    Ⓑ False

132. Plate armor is unbreakable.

Ⓐ True
Ⓑ False

133. The greatest disadvantage of body armor is its weight and inflexibility.

Ⓐ True
Ⓑ False

134. Choose the best vehicle to escape an infected city quickly and undetected.

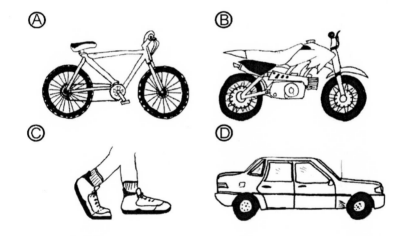

Ⓐ Letter A
Ⓑ Letter B
Ⓒ Letter C
Ⓓ Letter D

135. *Situation:* You and a teammate are being chased by zombies. The two of you are running towards a vehicle. You reach the vehicle long before your teammate. However, your teammate has the keys. What action should you take?

Ⓐ Try to hotwire the car
Ⓑ Go back and cover your teammate until you both reach the vehicle
Ⓒ Yell for him to throw you the keys
Ⓓ Get in the car and buckle up until he gets there

136. Choose the best vehicle to travel off road.

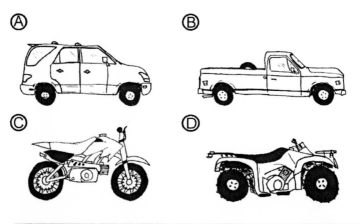

Ⓐ Letter A
Ⓑ Letter B
Ⓒ Letter C
Ⓓ Letter D

137. While scavenging/traveling, a large group of people (10+ people) is better than a small group of people (3-5 people).

Ⓐ True
Ⓑ False

138. It is best to travel at night because zombies cannot see you very well.

Ⓐ True
Ⓑ False

139. A freeway is one of the safest ways out of an infected area.

   Ⓐ True
   Ⓑ False

140. Which of the following vehicles has the best gas milage?

   Ⓐ Letter A
   Ⓑ Letter B
   Ⓒ Letter C
   Ⓓ Letter D

141. Never travel alone.

   Ⓐ True
   Ⓑ False

142. When in a rural area, traveling by foot is safer than driving.

   Ⓐ True
   Ⓑ False

143. *Situation:* Your friend is trapped in a car that is surrounded by hundreds of zombies. What action should take?

   Ⓐ Go back and attempt to rescue him
   Ⓑ Go on without him; there is nothing you can do

Ⓒ Try to get the zombies attention on you
Ⓓ Find other people to help you rescue him

144. Assuming you are traveling with 4+ people, which of the following vehicles would be worst in a zombie attack?

Ⓐ   Ⓑ

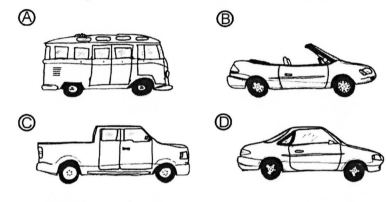

Ⓒ   Ⓓ

Ⓐ Letter A
Ⓑ Letter B
Ⓒ Letter C
Ⓓ Letter D

145. Large groups (10+ people) should all travel together in one vehicle, such as a bus.

Ⓐ True
Ⓑ False

146. Traveling underground is safer than traveling above ground.

Ⓐ True
Ⓑ False

147. The motorcycle is one of the best ways to travel during an outbreak.

Ⓐ True
Ⓑ False

148. Assuming you are traveling with 6+ people, which of the following vehicles would be the best in a zombie attack?

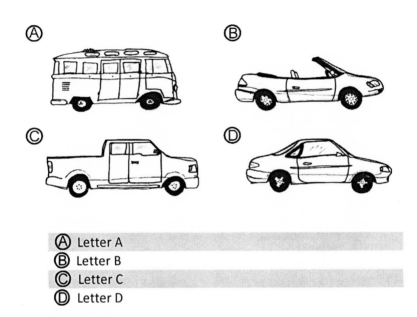

Ⓐ Letter A
Ⓑ Letter B
Ⓒ Letter C
Ⓓ Letter D

149. *Situation:* You are attempting to escape a heavily infected area in your car. However, about 1 mile ahead, you see a horde of zombies flooding the only road out of the area. What action do you take?

Ⓐ Go back and try to find another way out
Ⓑ Stay where you are until the zombie horde disperses
Ⓒ Drive through the zombie horde as fast as you can
Ⓓ Drive through the zombie horde, but push through the horde gently

150. A bicycle is a good vehicle to use to escape undetected.

Ⓐ True
Ⓑ False

151. Which of the following vehicles is the best for winter driving?

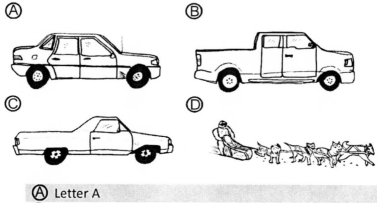

Ⓐ Letter A
Ⓑ Letter B
Ⓒ Letter C
Ⓓ Letter D

152. The better vehicle of choice is a minivan rather than a four door sedan.

Ⓐ True
Ⓑ False

153. Which of the following tire treads is the best for winter?

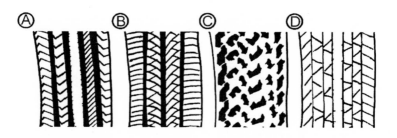

Ⓐ Letter A
Ⓑ Letter B
Ⓒ Letter C
Ⓓ Letter D

154. Which of the following vehicles is best for traveling through the woods?

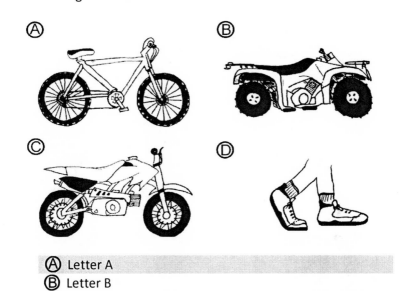

(A) Letter A
(B) Letter B
(C) Letter C
(D) Letter D

155. Most roads and freeways will be blocked and/or destroyed when escaping an infected area.

(A) True
(B) False

156. How many miles per hour can the average person travel by bicycle.

(A) 5-7
(B) 10-15
(C) 17-20
(D) 20+

157. Which of the following vehicles is the best for traveling through the desert?

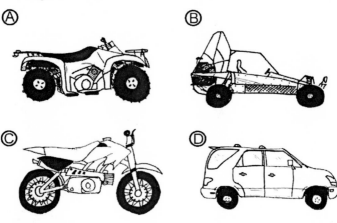

Ⓐ Letter A
Ⓑ Letter B
Ⓒ Letter C
Ⓓ Letter D

158. Dirt roads are the safest roads to travel on.

Ⓐ True
Ⓑ False

159. Which of the following is the best way to travel in your vehicle?

Ⓐ Letter A
Ⓑ Letter B
Ⓒ Letter C
Ⓓ Letter D

160. A disadvantage to riding a bicycle is the noise factor.

Ⓐ True
Ⓑ False

161. Even if you are an inexperienced rider, horseback riding is a good way to travel.

Ⓐ True
Ⓑ False

162. Which of the following roads is the safest to travel on?

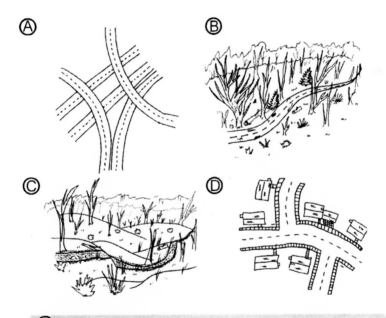

Ⓐ Letter A
Ⓑ Letter B
Ⓒ Letter C
Ⓓ Letter D

163. The type of tires on a vehicle does not matter.

Ⓐ True
Ⓑ False

164. If separated from your group members with no long range form of communication, it is best to yell out to them so they can find you.

Ⓐ True
Ⓑ False

165. Which of the following roads is the most dangerous to travel on?

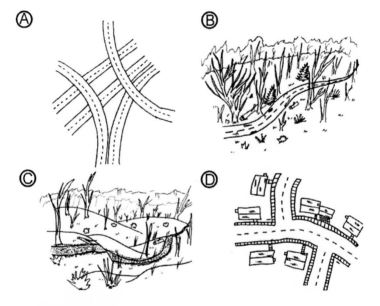

Ⓐ Letter A
Ⓑ Letter B
Ⓒ Letter C
Ⓓ Letter D

166. A large group (10+ people) is highly encouraged.

Ⓐ True
Ⓑ False

167. How many miles per hour can the average person travel on foot?

 Ⓐ 1
 Ⓑ 3
 Ⓒ 10
 Ⓓ 15

168. Which of the following aircraft is the safest form of air travel?

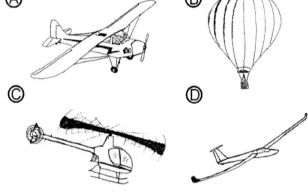

Ⓐ   Ⓑ

Ⓒ   Ⓓ

 Ⓐ Letter A
 Ⓑ Letter B
 Ⓒ Letter C
 Ⓓ Letter D

169. You should keep a campfire burning during the night to keep away the wild life.

 Ⓐ True
 Ⓑ False

170. When in combat, you should always keep moving.

 Ⓐ True
 Ⓑ False

171. Which of the following aircraft is the most efficient and practical transportation method during a zombie outbreak?

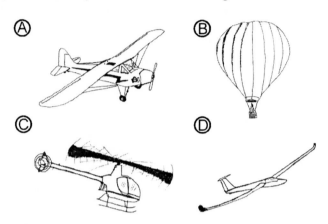

   Ⓐ Letter A
   Ⓑ Letter B
   Ⓒ Letter C
   Ⓓ Letter D

172. It is better to spend the night in a tent than in a vehicle.

   Ⓐ True
   Ⓑ False

173. A bicycle is not a good way to travel through an infected area.

   Ⓐ True
   Ⓑ False

174. Small groups (3-5 people) are the most efficient teams.

   Ⓐ True
   Ⓑ False

175. Which of the following water vessels is the safest means of marine travel during a zombie outbreak?

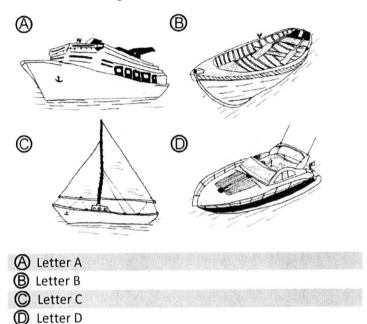

Ⓐ Letter A
Ⓑ Letter B
Ⓒ Letter C
Ⓓ Letter D

176. Which of the following water vessels is the fastest means of marine travel during a zombie outbreak?

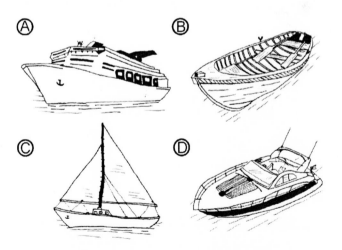

(A) Letter A
(B) Letter B
(C) Letter C
(D) Letter D

177. When escaping an infected area, it is best to travel with no supplies so they do not slow you down.

(A) True
(B) False

178. Always having a backup plan is key for survival.

(A) True
(B) False

179. What is the most important resource to have in your house during a zombie outbreak?

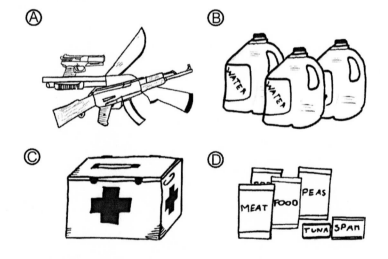

(A) Guns
(B) Water
(C) Medical supplies
(D) Canned goods

180. *Situation*: You have taken refuge in your house or apartment for months since the outbreak. You finally run out of food and water. What action should you take?

    (A) Cautiously travel to the nearest market and bring food and water back
    (B) Find another house/apartment with food, water, supplies, and live there
    (C) Just wait a little longer until you make any decisions, somebody might come to rescue you soon
    (D) Loot from the next door neighbors who have abandoned their residents

181. When packing supplies for travel, it is better to have matches than a lighter.

    (A) True
    (B) False

182. When packing supplies for travel, a flashlight is better than a lantern.

    (A) True
    (B) False

183. When packing supplies for travel, a hand held television is better than a hand held radio.

    (A) True
    (B) False

184. A disadvantage of canned goods is that they expire to fast.

    (A) True
    (B) False

185. When traveling, which of the following items is needed the least?

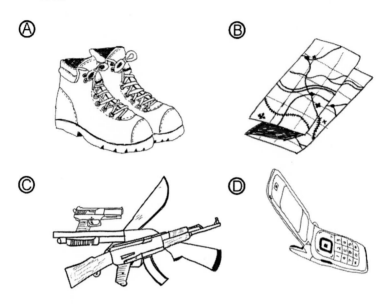

Ⓐ Letter A
Ⓑ Letter B
Ⓒ Letter C
Ⓓ Letter D

186. Cell phones are the best way to communicate with other members of your group when separated.

Ⓐ True
Ⓑ False

187. Two-way/CB radios are the best way to communicate with other members of your group when separated.

Ⓐ True
Ⓑ False

188. When traveling, which of the following items is needed the most?

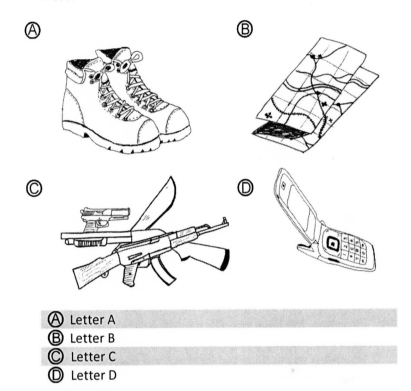

Ⓐ Letter A
Ⓑ Letter B
Ⓒ Letter C
Ⓓ Letter D

189. When packing supplies for travel, a map and compass are better than a GPS.

Ⓐ True
Ⓑ False

190. Binoculars are not necessary when packing supplies for travel.

Ⓐ True
Ⓑ False

191. When traveling using a motorcycle or dirt bike, which of the following items is needed least?

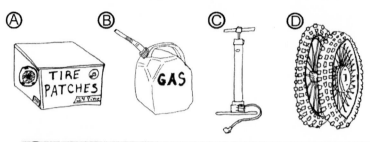

ⓐ Letter A
ⓑ Letter B
ⓒ Letter C
ⓓ Letter D

192. Dehydration can be just as dangerous as zombies.

ⓐ True
ⓑ False

193. *Situation:* You have not eaten much food in the last several days and you find a large supply of canned goods. However, according to the label the food expired several months ago. What action should you take?

ⓐ Do not eat it; food poisoning is not something you can risk
ⓑ Find something better in the next few days
ⓒ Eat it; canned goods can last a lot longer than the label says
ⓓ Come back if you do not find anything in the next few days

194. MREs (Meal, Ready-to-Eat) have a shelf life of 5-10 years.

ⓐ True
ⓑ False

195. A pocket knife is not a necessary tool to carry.

Ⓐ True
Ⓑ False

196. When traveling using a motorcycle or dirt bike, which of the following items is needed most?

Ⓐ Letter A
Ⓑ Letter B
Ⓒ Letter C
Ⓓ Letter D

197. Sugar based food products will provide you with long lasting energy.

Ⓐ True
Ⓑ False

198. Always choose energy drinks over water.

Ⓐ True
Ⓑ False

199. When packing food supplies for traveling, canned goods are better than MREs or freeze-dried foods.

Ⓐ True
Ⓑ False

200. Polarized sunglasses are not better than regular sunglasses.

   Ⓐ True
   Ⓑ False

201. Generally, houses are safer than apartments.

   Ⓐ True
   Ⓑ False

202. You must drink as little water as possible.

   Ⓐ True
   Ⓑ False

203. Zombies are the only thing you should worry about when an outbreak occurs.

   Ⓐ True
   Ⓑ False

204. *Situation:* You are being evacuated from the city for some unknown reason, and someone tries to car jack you at gun point. What action should you take?

   Ⓐ Fight back; you know your only chance of survival is to leave the city
   Ⓑ Do not fight back, give him the car; there is no point in dying over it
   Ⓒ Tell him that he can join you in the car
   Ⓓ Try to escape by driving off

205. In times of emergency, people are rational and in control.

   Ⓐ True
   Ⓑ False

206. During an outbreak, everyone will be focused and calm.

Ⓐ True
Ⓑ False

207. *Situation:* You are walking alone through a zombie-infested town. You see a sign on a house that says, "SAFE INSIDE!" What action should you take?

Ⓐ Ignore it and keep on going cautiously; it could be a trap set by other survivors
Ⓑ Go investigate, but be very cautious
Ⓒ Knock on the door and introduce yourself
Ⓓ Ignore it and keep going, but go back if it gets too late and you need shelter

208. *Situation:* You have been traveling alone for the duration of the zombie outbreak. Finally, you meet other survivors. What action do you take?

Ⓐ Be friendly and welcoming, not hostile
Ⓑ Arm yourself and be very cautious, but civil
Ⓒ Turn around and run away
Ⓓ Be aggressive and demanding

209. In times of emergency, it will be easy to convince and motivate people to do what you want.

Ⓐ True
Ⓑ False

210. It is highly encouraged to share as much personal information about yourself with strangers.

Ⓐ True
Ⓑ False

211. *Situation:* It has been months since the outbreak occurred and you are taking refuge in your house. You see a helicopter flying overhead. What action should you take?

   Ⓐ Try to signal it with anything you have (gunfire, flares, smoke, etc.)
   Ⓑ Follow it in a vehicle to see where it lands
   Ⓒ Let it go and do nothing. It is too dangerous to try to signal it
   Ⓓ Let it go, but make a large "HELP" sign to signal it if it returns

212. When camping in the woods overnight during a zombie outbreak, zombies are not your only fear.

   Ⓐ True
   Ⓑ False

213. Wild life and other survivors should not be a primary concern.

   Ⓐ True
   Ⓑ False

214. It is important to keep your group motivated and positive.

   Ⓐ True
   Ⓑ False

215. Short hair is better than long hair.

   Ⓐ True
   Ⓑ False

216. Which of the following is the preferred hair cut?

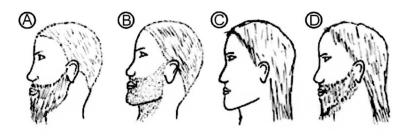

Ⓐ Letter A
Ⓑ Letter B
Ⓒ Letter C
Ⓓ Letter D

217. If you are dehydrated and have very little water, it is best to drink small amounts at a time and make it last as long as possible.

Ⓐ True
Ⓑ False

218. Short naps are better than a long nights sleep.

Ⓐ True
Ⓑ False

219. What part of your body is most likely to get bitten by a zombie?

Ⓐ Face
Ⓑ Neck
Ⓒ Leg
Ⓓ Arm

220. Which of the following is the best body type?

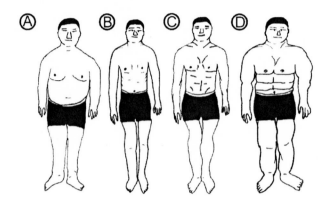

(A) Letter A
(B) Letter B
(C) Letter C
(D) Letter D

221. Staying awake as much as possible is key to surviving.

(A) True
(B) False

222. If you cannot sleep, use sleeping pills.

(A) True
(B) False

223. Being physically fit before a zombie outbreak is not essential.

(A) True
(B) False

224. A healthy diet is essential.

(A) True
(B) False

225. In order for you and your group members to survive, you must not allow your emotions to get the best of you.

Ⓐ True
Ⓑ False

226. Which of the following is the worst body type?

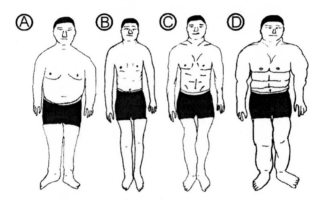

Ⓐ Letter A
Ⓑ Letter B
Ⓒ Letter C
Ⓓ Letter D

227. Being under the age of 40 is an advantage.

Ⓐ True
Ⓑ False

228. Non-smokers have a higher chance of survival than smokers.

Ⓐ True
Ⓑ False

229. It is necessary to have a positive mental attitude.

Ⓐ True
Ⓑ False

230. It is not necessary to always be alert.

   Ⓐ True
   Ⓑ False

231. It is important to have a negative mental attitude.

   Ⓐ True
   Ⓑ False

232. *Situation:* You hear several news reports on the television about small riots and wild attacks in your area. What action should you take?

   Ⓐ Ignore it; there is no need for concern
   Ⓑ Watch the news very careful over the next several days
   Ⓒ Prepare for the worst and take extreme precautions
   Ⓓ Drive to the scene and investigate the matter personally

233. Having camping skills prior to a zombie outbreak is not a necessary skill to have in order to survive.

   Ⓐ True
   Ⓑ False

234. *Situation:* You hear on the local news that the hospital is filled to capacity with sick patients. Soon after the report, the military arrives. What action should you take?

   Ⓐ Start fortifying your house/apartment
   Ⓑ Leave the area immediately with all the survival supplies you need
   Ⓒ Do nothing unless things get worse or the military gives the public specific orders to take
   Ⓓ Leave the area immediately and leave everything behind-- every second counts

235. *Situation:* You are trapped on the third floor of an office building. The room has no windows and only one door. You can hear a horde of zombies outside the door. What action should you take?

Ⓐ Try to run out of the room before more zombies arrive
Ⓑ Sit and wait for rescue or for the zombies to leave
Ⓒ Yell for help so a teammate can come to your aid
Ⓓ Open the door and shoot each zombie as it enters the room

236. Cemeteries are the worst place to be in a zombie attack.

Ⓐ True
Ⓑ False

237. As soon as an outbreak begins and reaches your area, what is the first thing you should do after locking your doors?

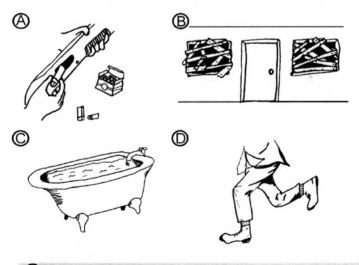

Ⓐ Load guns
Ⓑ Board up windows
Ⓒ Fill up bathtub with water
Ⓓ Run

238. Generally, your house (if not in the city) is one of the safest places to stay during a zombie outbreak.

    (A) True
    (B) False

239. If your current residence is outside the city limits, the first thing you should do is leave when an outbreak occurs.

    (A) True
    (B) False

240. *Situation:* You and your team want to take refuge in a house for the night. The doors and windows are all locked, and no one appears to be home. What action should you take?

    (A) Break open a door or window and go in
    (B) Knock first and listen very closely
    (C) Try to find a different house with the doors unlocked
    (D) Knock and listen, break open the door or window, and cautiously check every room

241. Your chances of survival during an outbreak will depend on where you live.

    (A) True
    (B) False

242. You are safer from zombies when at sea instead of on land.

    (A) True
    (B) False

243. *Situation:* You and your team have decided to make camp in the middle of the woods. It is your turn to take watch. At about 2:00 a.m. you hear faint sounds coming from the darkness. What action should you take?

Ⓐ Immediately go investigate the sound alone because you do not want to wake anybody

Ⓑ Wait for the sound to get louder or closer until you inform everybody

Ⓒ Wake everybody up to inform them that you heard a sound

Ⓓ Go investigate alone if the sound gets louder or closer

244. Which of the following is the best house to take refuge in during an outbreak?

Ⓐ Letter A
Ⓑ Letter B
Ⓒ Letter C
Ⓓ Letter D

245. Urban areas are safe locations to take refuge.

Ⓐ True
Ⓑ False

246. When staying in your home during an outbreak, using only the second floor and destroying the stairs is the smartest and best way to stay safe.

   (A) True
   (B) False

247. What is wrong with this picture?

   (A) Nothing
   (B) No need to board up the second story windows, use them as your exit
   (C) Need more boards on all the windows and doors
   (D) Do not board up the door, it provides a fast escape in an emergency

248. Depending on where you live, knowing multiple languages would be a useful skill to possess.

   (A) True
   (B) False

249. *Situation:* You live about 20 miles from the nearest city. You hear that they have quarantined the city because of a deadly virus outbreak. What action should you take?

    Ⓐ Leave your house immediately with all the survival supplies you need

    Ⓑ Leave your house immediately and leave everything behind-- every second counts

    Ⓒ Do nothing until the news or military issue specific orders

    Ⓓ Fortify your house and take refuge there

250. It is not important to know every single thing about a new area that you are traveling into.

    Ⓐ True

    Ⓑ False

251. When on a boat, staying as close to shore as possible is the safest course of action.

    Ⓐ True

    Ⓑ False

252. *Situation:* You live in the city and hear that it is being evacuated. What action should you take?

    Ⓐ Evacuate immediately with all the survival supplies you need

    Ⓑ Stay in the city and fortify your house/apartment

    Ⓒ Evacuate immediately, leave everything behind-- every second counts

    Ⓓ Loot nearby food and gun stores, then fortify your house/apartment

253. If your backyard is secure, which of the following is the most important?

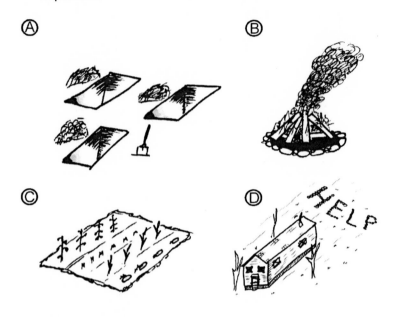

Ⓐ Digging graves
Ⓑ Starting a smoke signal
Ⓒ Growing a garden
Ⓓ Building a "HELP" sign

254. *Situation:* Several hours after the outbreak you take refuge in your house alone and secure all the doors and windows. However, you are very concerned about the safety of your friends and family. What action should you take?

Ⓐ Leave immediately to rescue them and bring them back to your house
Ⓑ Leave immediately but stay at their house
Ⓒ Leave to rescue them after a few days when things calm down
Ⓓ Hope that their safe and okay, but stay in your house

255. Choose the best place to go when an outbreak occurs.

Ⓐ Church
Ⓑ Hospital
Ⓒ Supermarket
Ⓓ Your House

256. *Situation:* You and your team have decided to make camp next to a lake. In the far distance you see a body moving out on the water. You have a few more hours until it is dark. What action should you take?

Ⓐ Leave it alone, it is too far away to reach you
Ⓑ Move camp location further away from lake
Ⓒ Walk around the lake as a team to get a closer look then make a decision
Ⓓ Swim out to investigate the body closer and kill if it is a zombie

257. If in desperate need of food or supplies, you should travel into the nearest city to get them because you will have a greater chance of finding what you need.

Ⓐ True
Ⓑ False

258. Choose the worst place to go when an outbreak occurs?

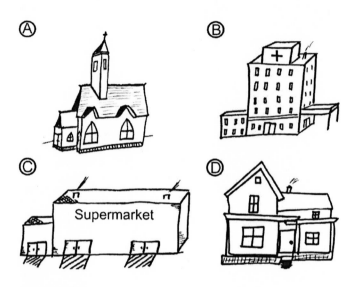

Ⓐ Church
Ⓑ Hospital
Ⓒ Supermarket
Ⓓ Your House

259. If you live in the city and are well armed, well stocked, and well protected, you still have little chance of surviving.

Ⓐ True
Ⓑ False

260. *Situation:* One of your teammates was injured in an accident. The other teammates want to take him to the nearest hospital to get medical supplies. What action should you take?

Ⓐ Go to the nearest hospital and get medical supplies as a team
Ⓑ One person go to the nearest hospital and gets medical supplies

© Do not go to the hospital and find medical supplies someplace else

© Do nothing and use whatever supplies you have

261. If you are taking refuge in the second story of your house, what is wrong with this picture?

(First Story)

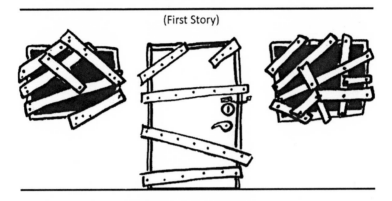

Ⓐ Nothing

Ⓑ Windows should not be boarded up

© Door should not be boarded up, better for escape

Ⓓ Dead bolt is not locked

262. It is unsafe if you have bars on your house windows.

Ⓐ True

Ⓑ False

263. *Situation:* You and your team have just escaped an infected area and are now traveling through the woods. Everyone in the group is dehydrated and you come upon a freshwater stream. What action should you take?

Ⓐ Immediately drink it and keep on moving

Ⓑ Boil the water, drink it, and then keep on moving

© Make camp and drink it, there is no need to boil freshwater

Ⓓ Make camp, boil the water, and then drink it

264. When sweeping an area, which of the following is the best
method of retrieving a zombie from a body of water?

Ⓐ   Ⓑ

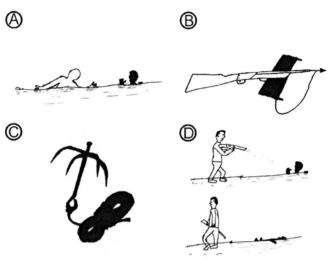

Ⓒ   Ⓓ

Ⓐ Swim out to it and bring it back to shore
Ⓑ Use a spear gun
Ⓒ Use a grappling hook
Ⓓ Just shoot it in the head and leave it out there

265. In the case of a large outbreak, cities stand the chance of
being bombed or incinerated.

Ⓐ True
Ⓑ False

266. The desert is one of the safest places to take shelter from
zombies.

Ⓐ True
Ⓑ False

267. There is no need to lock your doors during a zombie
outbreak because zombies cannot open doors.

Ⓐ True
Ⓑ False

268. Which of the following areas should be avoided the most?

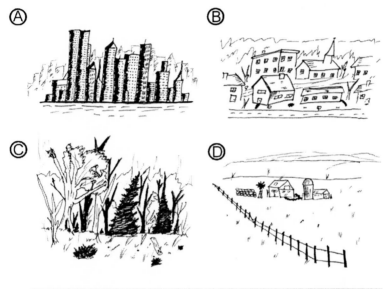

Ⓐ Letter A
Ⓑ Letter B
Ⓒ Letter C
Ⓓ Letter D

269. *Situation:* You have enough food and water to last for several more months. You hear a repeated transmission on your radio about a safe military base 30 miles away. What action should you take?

Ⓐ Just stay in your house, there is no reason to take the risk
Ⓑ Leave immediately with all the survival supplies you need
Ⓒ Leave in a few days so you can prepare yourself for the trip
Ⓓ Try to signal for help from the house with flares or smoke signals

270. Which of the following areas is the best to take refuge in?

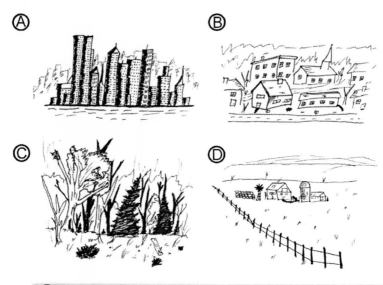

Ⓐ Letter A
Ⓑ Letter B
Ⓒ Letter C
Ⓓ Letter D

271. *Situation:* You are attempting to leave the city when the evacuation is declared. However, by the time you reach the border of the city, the military has quarantined you inside, and will not allow anybody to leave. What action do you take?

Ⓐ Return to your house or apartment and wait for the crisis to end
Ⓑ Loot nearby food and gun stores, then fortify your house/apartment
Ⓒ Try to find another way out of the city no matter what
Ⓓ Return to your house or apartment and immediately fortify yourself inside

272. Staying in your house is not safe, always keep moving.

    Ⓐ True
    Ⓑ False

273. *Situation:* You are taking refuge in your house when the zombie outbreak occurs. The news says to board up your doors and windows. However, you do not have the boards or supplies to barricade yourself inside. What action do you take?

    Ⓐ Go outside and find supplies
    Ⓑ Drive to the nearest hardware store and get some supplies
    Ⓒ Use large items around the house to barricade the doors and windows
    Ⓓ Do nothing, just lock the doors and windows

274. It is better to take refuge in the first story of a house than the second story.

    Ⓐ True
    Ⓑ False

275. You are taking refuge on the second story of your house. What do you do with the staircase?

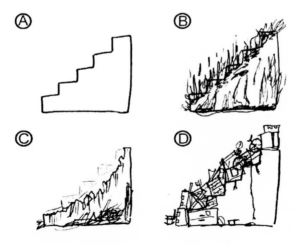

Ⓐ Leave it alone, provides easier access to both stories
Ⓑ Burn it down
Ⓒ Cut it down
Ⓓ Block it off with household items

276. You will be 100% safe camping overnight in a tree.

Ⓐ True
Ⓑ False

277. When camping in the woods overnight during a zombie outbreak, it is best for another group member to stay awake and keep watch.

Ⓐ True
Ⓑ False

278. If camping alone in the woods overnight during a zombie outbreak, you should consider taking refuge off the ground, such as in a tree.

Ⓐ True
Ⓑ False

279. When taking refuge in a house, where is the best location to defend yourself with firepower against a horde of zombies?

Ⓐ Basement
Ⓑ First story
Ⓒ Second story
Ⓓ Rooftop

280. Which of the following is the best type of house to take refuge in?

Ⓐ Frame houses
Ⓑ Log houses
Ⓒ Stone or concrete houses
Ⓓ Depends on the location

281. When taking refuge in your house during an outbreak, you should consider starting a garden outside for food.

   Ⓐ True
   Ⓑ False

282. When taking refuge in your house during an outbreak, it is strongly discouraged to have a pet for companionship (i.e. dog or cat).

   Ⓐ True
   Ⓑ False

283. *Situation:* It is winter and you see a frozen zombie corpse near your house or camp. What action should you take?

   Ⓐ Leave it alone, do not take the chance of getting infected
   Ⓑ Take care of it in the spring
   Ⓒ Go outside and kill it before spring arrives
   Ⓓ Do not worry about it, zombies and the virus die when frozen

284. Which of the following is the best clothing to wear in the summer when traveling?

   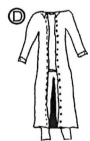

   Ⓐ Letter A
   Ⓑ Letter B
   Ⓒ Letter C
   Ⓓ Letter D

285. *Situation:* It is autumn, you are walking through the woods, and you hear the sound of footsteps on the dried leaves. What action should you take?

Ⓐ Stay alert and cautious, have primary weapon in hand and prepared
Ⓑ Run in the opposite direction of the sound
Ⓒ Stand still and wait until the sound quits or you see what is making it
Ⓓ Walk towards the sound very quietly

286. Zombies cannot survive in snow.

Ⓐ True
Ⓑ False

287. It is safer to travel during the winter than summer.

Ⓐ True
Ⓑ False

288. Which of the following is the best clothing to wear in the winter when traveling?

Ⓐ Letter A
Ⓑ Letter B
Ⓒ Letter C
Ⓓ Letter D

289. *Situation:* You are taking refuge in your house when the zombie outbreak occurs. It is the middle of winter and you are freezing from the cold and snow. You want to make a fire in the fireplace but are afraid of attracting zombies or other survivors to your house. What action do you take?

Ⓐ Make the fire, there is no reason for you to freeze
Ⓑ Try to keep warm in different ways, you do not want to attract anything
Ⓒ *Suck it up*, it will be over soon
Ⓓ Drink alcohol, it will warm your body

290. Incineration is the worst way to dispose of a zombie corpse.

Ⓐ True
Ⓑ False

291. What is the best way to dispose of a zombie's corpse?

Ⓐ Bury
Ⓑ Incineration
Ⓒ Just leave it alone
Ⓓ None of the above

292. Burying a dead body is the best way to dispose of a zombie corpse.

Ⓐ True
Ⓑ False

PERSONAL EVALATION:

1. What sex are you?

    Ⓐ Male
    Ⓑ Female

2. What is your body type?

    Ⓐ Slender
    Ⓑ Average
    Ⓒ Muscular
    Ⓓ Overweight

3. What age are you?

    Ⓐ 0-17
    Ⓑ 18-29
    Ⓒ 30-59
    Ⓓ 60 or Over

4. How long is your hair?

    Ⓐ Bald/Short
    Ⓑ Average
    Ⓒ Shoulder Length
    Ⓓ Below Shoulders

5. What is your highest level of education?

    Ⓐ High School Diploma/GED
    Ⓑ Some College
    Ⓒ Bachelors Degree
    Ⓓ Advanced/Professional Degree

6. Choose the best description for your typical sleep pattern.

    Ⓐ Light sleeper; anything can wake you up
    Ⓑ Moderate sleeper; any loud sound or a shake will wake
       you up

Ⓒ Heavy sleeper; very difficult to wake
Ⓓ All the above; sleeping pattern is very random

7. Level of hands-on survival experience?

Ⓐ Very little/none
Ⓑ Some experience
Ⓒ A lot of experience
Ⓓ Expert

8. Level of hands-on firearm experience?

Ⓐ Very little/none
Ⓑ Some experience
Ⓒ A lot of experience
Ⓓ Expert

9. Do you own any firearms?

Ⓐ Yes
Ⓑ No

10. Level of hands-on experience with blades
(swords/machetes/knifes)?

Ⓐ Very little/none
Ⓑ Some experience
Ⓒ A lot of experience
Ⓓ Expert

11. Level of hands-on experience with vehicles?

Ⓐ Very little/none
Ⓑ Some experience
Ⓒ A lot of experience
Ⓓ Expert

12. Level of hands-on experience with vehicle repair/maintenance?

(A) Very little/none
(B) Some experience
(C) A lot of experience
(D) Expert

13. Level of hands-on climbing experience?

(A) Very little/none
(B) Some experience
(C) A lot of experience
(D) Expert

14. Level of hands-on combat training?

(A) Very little/none
(B) Some experience
(C) A lot of experience
(D) Expert

15. Where do you currently reside?

(A) City
(B) Town
(C) Country
(D) Woods, mountains, desert, etc

16. Do you own a horse? If so, are you an experienced rider?

(A) No and no
(B) Yes, but I am not an experienced rider
(C) I am an experienced rider, but do not own a horse
(D) Yes and yes

17. Do you own a vehicle?

(A) Yes
(B) No

18. Can you drive?

    Ⓐ Yes
    Ⓑ No

19. Can you drive a standard/manual vehicle?

    Ⓐ Yes
    Ⓑ No

20. Can you run for an extended period of time (2+ miles without stopping)?

    Ⓐ Yes
    Ⓑ No

21. What is your relationship status?

    Ⓐ Single with no children
    Ⓑ Married with no children
    Ⓒ Single with children
    Ⓓ Married with children

22. Which of the following do you reside in?

    Ⓐ House
    Ⓑ Apartment (single or half house)
    Ⓒ Apartment Complex
    Ⓓ College Dorm/Other

23. How many stories/levels is your house or apartment?

    Ⓐ One
    Ⓑ Two or more

24. Do you have military experience?

    Ⓐ Yes
    Ⓑ No

25. Have you ever taken another person's life?

Ⓐ Yes
Ⓑ No

26. Are you currently pregnant?

Ⓐ Yes
Ⓑ No

27. Are you disabled or handicapped in any way?

Ⓐ Yes
Ⓑ No

28. How many limbs do you have?

Ⓐ 4
Ⓑ 3
Ⓒ 2
Ⓓ 1-0

29. Do you have any medical experience, such as training in first-aid or CPR?

Ⓐ Yes
Ⓑ No

30. How often do you exercise/work out?

Ⓐ Very little to none
Ⓑ Several times a year
Ⓒ Several times a month
Ⓓ Several times a week

31. Do you actively participate in gymnastics or any other form of aerobics?

Ⓐ Yes
Ⓑ No

32. In the event of an outbreak, would you follow the speed limit?

    (A) Yes
    (B) No

33. Are you a smoker? If so, how much?

    (A) No
    (B) Yes, very little, a few cigarettes every week or longer
    (C) Yes, moderate, one pack a week
    (D) Yes, heavy, more than one pack a week

34. Are you a moderate to heavy drinker?

    (A) Yes
    (B) No

35. Do you drink and drive on a regular basis?

    (A) Yes
    (B) No

36. Do you know how to treat a broken bone?

    (A) Yes
    (B) No

37. Do you know how to stop bleeding?

    (A) Yes
    (B) No

38. Do you know how to use a tourniquet?

    (A) Yes
    (B) No

39. Do you know how to treat burns properly?

    Ⓐ Yes
    Ⓑ No

40. Do you know how to swim?

    Ⓐ Yes
    Ⓑ No

41. Do you use drugs on a regular basis (prescription or illegal)?

    Ⓐ Yes
    Ⓑ No

42. Do you know the signs of frostbite?

    Ⓐ Yes
    Ⓑ No

43. Do you know how to treat frostbite?

    Ⓐ Yes
    Ⓑ No

44. Do you know the signs of food poisoning?

    Ⓐ Yes
    Ⓑ No

45. Do you know how to treat food poisoning?

    Ⓐ Yes
    Ⓑ No

46. Do you know the signs of heat exhaustion?

    Ⓐ Yes
    Ⓑ No

47. Do you know how to treat heat exhaustion?

Ⓐ Yes
Ⓑ No

48. Do you know how to treat heat stroke or sunstroke?

Ⓐ Yes
Ⓑ No

49. Do you know the signs of infection?

Ⓐ Yes
Ⓑ No

50. Do you know how to treat an infection?

Ⓐ Yes
Ⓑ No

51. Do you know how to properly dress a wound?

Ⓐ Yes
Ⓑ No

52. Do you know how to purify water?

Ⓐ Yes
Ⓑ No

53. Are you diabetic?

Ⓐ Yes
Ⓑ No

54. Do you have a history of heart attacks or heart failure?

Ⓐ Yes
Ⓑ No

55. Do you have any hands-on experience with operating an airplane?

 (A) Yes
 (B) No

56. Do you have any hands-on experience with operating a helicopter?

 (A) Yes
 (B) No

57. Do you have any hands-on experience with operating a boat?

 (A) Yes
 (B) No

58. How many miles is the nearest gun and ammo store to your house/apartment?

 (A) 1-5 miles
 (B) 6-10 miles
 (C) 11-20 miles
 (D) 21+ miles/Do not know

59. Do you prefer to work alone or as a team?

 (A) Alone
 (B) Team

60. Have you ever hunted large game?

 (A) Yes
 (B) No

STOP

**THIS IS THE END OF THE
ZOMBIE SURVIVAL APTITUDE TEST**

<u>**DO NOT CHANGE ANY ANSWERS PAST THIS POINT!**</u>

SCORING GUIDE:

Use the following scoring guide to calculate your final grade.

POINT SCALE:

The following types of question have different point scales. If your letter answer corresponds with the letter answer in the following scoring guide, than you will receive full credit for the answer. If your letter answer **does not** correspond with the letter answer in the scoring guide, than you will receive zero credit.

1. **Fact Based Multiple Choice:**
   Correct answers will receive **4 points**.
   Semi-correct answers will receive **2 points**.
   Incorrect answers will receive **0 points**.

2. **Situational Multiple Choice:**
   Correct answers will receive **4 points**.
   Semi-correct answers will receive **2 points**.
   Incorrect answers will receive **0 points**.

3. **Situational Illustration Multiple Choice:**
   Correct answers will receive **4 points**.
   Semi-correct answers will receive **2 points**.
   Incorrect answers will receive **0 points**.

4. **True and False:**
   Correct answers will receive **2 points**.
   Incorrect answers will receive **0 points**.

5. **Personal Evaluation:**
   Point will vary from **6, 4, 2, 0** depending on your strengths and weaknesses.

GRADING SCALE:

Expert: 100% - 90% (1.0 - .90)
Professional: 89% - 80% (.89 - .80)
Novice: 79% - 70% (.79 - .70)
Amateur: 69% - 60% (.69 - .60)
Minor: 59% and Under (.59 and Under)

DEFINING GRADING SCALE LEVELS:
Expert/Professional/Novice/Amateur/Minor

1. **Expert:** Highest rated individual with special skills and knowledge in the field of zombie survival. A zombie survival expert is the elite. They are widely accepted as an extremely reliable source of zombie survival techniques, skills, and experience that are virtually unheard of by most zombie survivalists.

    LIFE EXPECTANCY IN THE EVENT OF A ZOMBIE OUTBREAK: **1 or More Years**; an expert could expect to survive for a number of years without much difficulty. Their skills, knowledge, and instincts are so developed that practically nothing can get the better of them. They have planned out almost every type of problem, event, and contingency possible in their head long before an attack ever occurs. As a result, they react to situations on a much higher level than most people, and escape and/or solve any confrontation they are faced with.
    ★★★★★

2. **Professional:** High to moderate rated individual with skills and knowledge in the field of zombie survival. A zombie survival professional has a sufficient amount of knowledge and skills to defend against zombies for an extended period of time.

    LIFE EXPECTANCY IN THE EVENT OF A ZOMBIE OUTBREAK: **1-12 Months**; a professional could expect to survive for a number of months, unless they gain the additional skills, knowledge, and experience to be promoted to *expert* status. A professional knows all about zombie survival and has, in all probability, planned many different circumstances and situations in their head, but has not totally developed, polished, and perfected their abilities and talents. More work is needed in order for them to survive long in a full blown zombie outbreak. ★★★★

3. **Novice:** Moderate to low rated individual with little skills and knowledge in the field of zombie survival. A zombie survival novice does not have a sufficient amount of knowledge or skill to defend against zombie for an extended amount of time.

   LIFE EXPECTANCY IN THE EVENT OF A ZOMBIE OUTBREAK: **1-4 Weeks**; a novice is not expected to survive very long in the event of a zombie outbreak. They might have enough skills and knowledge to make a few escapes, but will not last long. Their survival is primarily based off luck and timing. However, this type of survival technique will not allow a novice to live long. Without sufficient skills and knowledge they will likely die in less than a month. A novice's only hope for survival is to partner with a professional or expert as soon as possible. ★★★

4. **Amateur:** Low rated individual with no skills or knowledge in the field of zombie survival. A zombie survival amateur has very little to no chance of surviving a zombie outbreak.

   LIFE EXPECTANCY IN THE EVENT OF A ZOMBIE OUTBREAK: **1-7 Days**; an amateur is not expected to survive longer than one week. The individuals that fall under this category will soon be new recruits for the zombie horde. The zombie survival amateur is where most of the zombie's numbers arise from. Their low level of skills and knowledge make them prime pray to the zombies. An amateur has very little to no chance of surviving a zombie outbreak even with the assistance of a professional or expert. ★★

5. **Minor:** Lowest rated individual with absolutely no skills, knowledge, or experience of any kind. They are usually the first to become zombies within the first 24 hours of a zombie outbreak.

   LIFE EXPECTANCY IN THE EVENT OF A ZOMBIE OUTBREAK: **1-24 Hours;** Minors are the catalyst of the virus and are primarily responsible for spreading the outbreak. These individuals probably had little to no warning of an outbreak and had no time to react or did not react appropriately. Minors are typically ignorant and do not take these events seriously. Nobody taking this Z-SAT should receive a minor rating. ★

FORMULA FOR CALCULATING GRADE PERCENTAGE:

Your Total Points ÷ 1230 (Max Points Possible) = .XX = XX% (Your Grade)

Example: 924 ÷ 1230 = .75 = 75% (Novice)

HOW TO SCORE YOUR WORK:

Use the scoring guide to compare the correct answers with your answers. Some questions have more than one acceptable answer. However, only the 100% correct answer will grant you full credit. Write **your score** in the empty boxes provided.

Example 1: You answered Ⓓ on a question.

The scoring guide shows the Ⓓ across from the 2, therefore you receive 2/4 points for answering the question semi-correctly.

Answer	Points	Your Points
Ⓐ Ⓓ	4 2	2

Figure 1

If you answered Ⓐ you would have received 4/4 points for answering the question 100% correctly. (See Figure 1)

Answer	Points	Your Points
Ⓐ Ⓒ Ⓑ Ⓓ	4 3 2 1	3

Figure 2

Example 2: You answered Ⓒ on a question. You would receive 3/4 points. (See Figure 2)

SCORING GUIDE

#	Answer	Points	Your Score	#	Answer	Points	Your Score
1	Ⓒ	4		24	Ⓑ	2	
2	Ⓐ	2		25	Ⓓ	4	
3	Ⓑ	2		26	Ⓑ	2	
4	Ⓐ	4		27	Ⓑ	2	
5	Ⓑ	2		28	Ⓑ	2	
6	Ⓐ	2		29	Ⓑ	2	
7	Ⓑ	2		30	Ⓐ	4	
8	Ⓓ Ⓑ or Ⓒ	4 2		31	Ⓑ	2	
9	Ⓑ	2		32	Ⓒ	4	
10	Ⓑ	2		33	Ⓑ	2	
11	Ⓐ	4		34	Ⓓ	4	
12	Ⓓ	4		35	Ⓑ	2	
13	Ⓑ	2		36	Ⓑ	2	
14	Ⓑ	2		37	Ⓑ	2	
15	Ⓑ	4		38	Ⓓ Ⓐ	4 2	
16	Ⓑ	2		39	Ⓑ	2	
17	Ⓑ	2		40	Ⓐ	2	
18	Ⓑ	2		41	Ⓑ	2	
19	Ⓑ	2		42	Ⓐ	4	
20	Ⓒ	4		43	Ⓑ	2	
21	Ⓑ	2		44	Ⓐ	2	
22	Ⓐ	2		45	Ⓓ Ⓒ	4 2	
23	Ⓑ	2		**Page #1 Total:**		118	

#	Answer	Points	Your Score	#	Answer	Points	Your Score
46	Ⓐ	2		69	Ⓑ Ⓒ	4 2	
47	Ⓐ	2		70	Ⓑ	2	
48	Ⓒ Ⓓ	4 2		71	Ⓓ	4	
49	Ⓐ	2		72	Ⓑ	2	
50	Ⓓ Ⓑ	4 2		73	Ⓐ Ⓒ	4 2	
51	Ⓑ	2		74	Ⓒ Ⓓ	4 2	
52	Ⓑ	2		75	Ⓐ Ⓒ or Ⓓ	4 2	
53	Ⓐ	2		76	Ⓐ Ⓒ	4 2	
54	Ⓓ	4		77	Ⓑ	2	
55	Ⓐ	2		78	Ⓒ Ⓑ	4 2	
56	Ⓐ Ⓑ or Ⓒ	4 2		79	Ⓑ	2	
57	Ⓑ	2		80	Ⓑ	2	
58	Ⓑ	2		81	Ⓓ	4	
59	Ⓐ	4		82	Ⓐ	4	
60	Ⓓ	4		83	Ⓓ Ⓒ	4 2	
61	Ⓓ	4		84	Ⓑ	2	
62	Ⓑ	4		85	Ⓓ Ⓐ or Ⓒ	4 2	
63	Ⓑ	2		86	Ⓑ Ⓐ	4 2	
64	Ⓑ Ⓐ	4 2		87	Ⓑ Ⓒ	4 2	
65	Ⓐ	2		88	Ⓑ	2	
66	Ⓒ Ⓐ or Ⓓ	4 2		89	Ⓓ Ⓐ or Ⓒ	4 2	
67	Ⓑ	2		90	Ⓓ Ⓐ	4 2	
68	Ⓓ Ⓑ	4 2		Page #2 Total:		142	

#	Answer	Points	Your Score	#	Answer	Points	Your Score
91	Ⓑ	4		114	Ⓒ Ⓐ	4 2	
92	Ⓓ Ⓑ	4 2		115	Ⓑ Ⓐ	4 2	
93	Ⓑ	4		116	Ⓑ	4	
94	Ⓑ	4		117	Ⓑ	4	
95	Ⓑ	4		118	Ⓐ	4	
96	Ⓑ	4		119	Ⓐ	4	
97	Ⓒ	4		120	Ⓐ	4	
98	Ⓐ	4		121	Ⓓ Ⓑ	4 2	
99	Ⓒ	4		122	Ⓓ	4	
100	Ⓓ Ⓑ or Ⓒ	4 2		123	Ⓑ	2	
101	Ⓑ	4		124	Ⓒ	4	
102	Ⓑ	4		125	Ⓑ Ⓐ	4 2	
103	Ⓐ Ⓓ	4 2		126	Ⓑ	2	
104	Ⓓ	4		127	Ⓑ	2	
105	Ⓑ	4		128	Ⓑ	2	
106	Ⓓ	4		129	Ⓐ	2	
107	Ⓐ Ⓓ	4 2		130	Ⓑ	2	
108	Ⓑ	4		131	Ⓑ	2	
109	Ⓒ	4		132	Ⓑ	2	
110	Ⓐ	4		133	Ⓐ	2	
111	Ⓓ Ⓐ	4 2		134	Ⓐ Ⓒ	4 2	
112	Ⓓ	4		135	Ⓑ Ⓓ	4 2	
113	Ⓐ	4			Page #3 Total:	162	

#	Answer	Points	Your Score	#	Answer	Points	Your Score
136	Ⓓ Ⓒ	4 2		159	Ⓒ	4	
137	Ⓑ	2		160	Ⓑ	2	
138	Ⓑ	2		161	Ⓑ	2	
139	Ⓐ	2		162	Ⓐ Ⓑ	4 2	
140	Ⓑ	4		163	Ⓑ	2	
141	Ⓐ	2		164	Ⓑ	2	
142	Ⓑ	2		165	Ⓓ	4	
143	Ⓑ Ⓓ	4 2		166	Ⓑ	2	
144	Ⓑ Ⓓ	4 2		167	Ⓑ	4	
145	Ⓑ	2		168	Ⓑ	4	
146	Ⓑ	2		169	Ⓑ	2	
147	Ⓑ	2		170	Ⓐ	2	
148	Ⓐ Ⓒ	4 2		171	Ⓒ	4	
149	Ⓓ Ⓑ	4 2		172	Ⓑ	2	
150	Ⓐ	2		173	Ⓑ	2	
151	Ⓑ	4		174	Ⓐ	2	
152	Ⓑ	2		175	Ⓒ	4	
153	Ⓑ	4		176	Ⓓ	4	
154	Ⓒ Ⓓ	4 2		177	Ⓑ	2	
155	Ⓐ	2		178	Ⓐ	2	
156	Ⓑ	4		179	Ⓑ	4	
157	Ⓑ Ⓐ	4 2		180	Ⓓ Ⓐ	4 2	
158	Ⓑ	2		**Page #4 Total:**		**132**	

#	Answer	Points	Your Score	#	Answer	Points	Your Score
181	Ⓑ	2		204	Ⓒ Ⓑ	4 2	
182	Ⓐ	2		205	Ⓑ	2	
183	Ⓑ	2		206	Ⓑ	2	
184	Ⓑ	2		207	Ⓐ	4	
185	Ⓓ	4		208	Ⓑ Ⓐ	4 2	
186	Ⓑ	2		209	Ⓑ	2	
187	Ⓐ	2		210	Ⓐ	2	
188	Ⓒ	4		211	Ⓓ Ⓒ	4 2	
189	Ⓐ	2		212	Ⓐ	2	
190	Ⓑ	2		213	Ⓑ	2	
191	Ⓒ Ⓐ	4 2		214	Ⓐ	2	
192	Ⓐ	2		215	Ⓐ	2	
193	Ⓒ	4		216	Ⓑ Ⓐ	4 2	
194	Ⓐ	2		217	Ⓑ	2	
195	Ⓑ	2		218	Ⓑ	2	
196	Ⓑ	4		219	Ⓓ Ⓒ	4 2	
197	Ⓑ	2		220	Ⓒ Ⓑ	4 2	
198	Ⓑ	2		221	Ⓑ	2	
199	Ⓑ	2		222	Ⓑ	2	
200	Ⓑ	2		223	Ⓑ	2	
201	Ⓐ	2		224	Ⓐ	2	
202	Ⓑ	2		225	Ⓐ	2	
203	Ⓑ	2		**Page #5 Total:**		114	

#	Answer	Points	Your Score	#	Answer	Points	Your Score
226	Ⓐ	4		249	Ⓓ Ⓐ	4 2	
227	Ⓐ	2		250	Ⓑ	2	
228	Ⓐ	2		251	Ⓑ	2	
229	Ⓐ	2		252	Ⓐ	4	
230	Ⓑ	2		253	Ⓒ Ⓓ	4 2	
231	Ⓑ	2		254	Ⓓ	4	
232	Ⓑ Ⓒ	4 2		255	Ⓓ	4	
233	Ⓑ	2		256	Ⓒ Ⓑ	4 2	
234	Ⓑ Ⓐ	4 2		257	Ⓑ	2	
235	Ⓑ Ⓓ	4 2		258	Ⓑ Ⓐ	4 2	
236	Ⓑ	2		259	Ⓐ	2	
237	Ⓒ	4		260	Ⓒ Ⓓ	4 2	
238	Ⓐ	2		261	Ⓓ	4	
239	Ⓑ	2		262	Ⓑ	2	
240	Ⓓ Ⓑ	4 2		263	Ⓑ	4	
241	Ⓐ	2		264	Ⓑ Ⓒ	4 2	
242	Ⓐ	2		265	Ⓐ	2	
243	Ⓑ Ⓒ	4 2		266	Ⓐ	2	
244	Ⓓ Ⓒ	4 2		267	Ⓑ	2	
245	Ⓑ	2		268	Ⓐ	4	
246	Ⓐ	2		269	Ⓐ	4	
247	Ⓑ	4		270	Ⓓ	4	
248	Ⓐ	2		**Page #6 Total:**		136	

#	Answer	Points	Your Score
271	Ⓒ Ⓓ	4 2	
272	Ⓑ	2	
273	Ⓒ	4	
274	Ⓑ	2	
275	Ⓒ Ⓓ	4 2	
276	Ⓑ	2	
277	Ⓐ	2	
278	Ⓐ	2	
279	Ⓓ Ⓒ	4 2	
280	Ⓒ	4	
281	Ⓐ	2	
282	Ⓑ	2	
283	Ⓒ Ⓐ	4 2	
284	Ⓑ Ⓐ	4 2	
285	Ⓐ Ⓒ	4 2	
286	Ⓑ	2	
287	Ⓑ	2	
288	Ⓒ	4	
289	Ⓐ Ⓑ	4 2	
290	Ⓑ	2	
291	Ⓑ	4	
292	Ⓑ	2	

| Page #7 Total: | 66 | | | Total (Pages: 1-7): | Total Points 870 | Your Total Score |

#	Answer	Points	Your Score	#	Answer	Points	Your Score
1	Ⓐ ⒝	6 / 2		24	Ⓐ Ⓑ	6 / 0	
2	Ⓑ Ⓒ / Ⓐ Ⓓ	6 2 / 4 0		25	Ⓐ Ⓑ	6 / 0	
3	Ⓑ Ⓐ / Ⓒ Ⓓ	6 2 / 4 0		26	Ⓑ Ⓐ	6 / 0	
4	Ⓐ Ⓒ / Ⓑ Ⓓ	6 2 / 4 0		27	Ⓑ Ⓐ	6 / 0	
5	Ⓓ Ⓑ / Ⓒ Ⓐ	6 2 / 4 0		28	Ⓐ Ⓒ / Ⓑ Ⓓ	6 2 / 4 0	
6	Ⓐ Ⓒ / Ⓑ Ⓓ	6 2 / 4 0		29	Ⓐ Ⓑ	6 / 0	
7	Ⓓ Ⓑ / Ⓒ Ⓐ	6 2 / 4 0		30	Ⓓ Ⓑ / Ⓒ Ⓐ	6 2 / 4 0	
8	Ⓓ Ⓑ / Ⓒ Ⓐ	6 2 / 4 0		31	Ⓐ Ⓑ	6 / 0	
9	Ⓐ Ⓑ	6 / 0		32	Ⓐ Ⓑ	6 / 0	
10	Ⓓ Ⓑ / Ⓒ Ⓐ	6 2 / 4 0		33	Ⓐ Ⓒ / Ⓑ Ⓓ	6 2 / 4 0	
11	Ⓓ Ⓑ / Ⓒ Ⓐ	6 2 / 4 0		34	Ⓑ Ⓐ	6 / 0	
12	Ⓓ Ⓑ / Ⓒ Ⓐ	6 2 / 4 0		35	Ⓑ Ⓐ	6 / 0	
13	Ⓓ Ⓑ / Ⓒ Ⓐ	6 2 / 4 0		36	Ⓐ Ⓑ	6 / 0	
14	Ⓓ Ⓑ / Ⓒ Ⓐ	6 2 / 4 0		37	Ⓐ Ⓑ	6 / 0	
15	Ⓓ Ⓑ / Ⓒ Ⓐ	6 2 / 4 0		38	Ⓐ Ⓑ	6 / 0	
16	Ⓓ Ⓑ / Ⓒ Ⓐ	6 2 / 4 0		39	Ⓐ Ⓑ	6 / 0	
17	Ⓐ Ⓑ	6 / 0		40	Ⓐ Ⓑ	6 / 0	
18	Ⓐ Ⓑ	6 / 0		41	Ⓑ Ⓐ	6 / 0	
19	Ⓐ Ⓑ	6 / 0		42	Ⓐ Ⓑ	6 / 0	
20	Ⓐ Ⓑ	6 / 0		43	Ⓐ Ⓑ	6 / 0	
21	Ⓐ Ⓒ / Ⓑ Ⓓ	6 2 / 4 0		44	Ⓐ Ⓑ	6 / 0	
22	Ⓐ Ⓒ / Ⓑ Ⓓ	6 2 / 4 0		45	Ⓐ Ⓑ	6 / 0	
23	Ⓑ Ⓐ	6 / 2		Page #8 Total:		270	

#	Answer	Points	Your Score
46	Ⓐ Ⓑ	6 0	
47	Ⓐ Ⓑ	6 0	
48	Ⓐ Ⓑ	6 0	
49	Ⓐ Ⓑ	6 0	
50	Ⓐ Ⓑ	6 0	
51	Ⓐ Ⓑ	6 0	
52	Ⓐ Ⓑ	6 0	
53	Ⓑ Ⓐ	6 0	
54	Ⓑ Ⓐ	6 0	
55	Ⓐ Ⓑ	6 0	
56	Ⓐ Ⓑ	6 0	
57	Ⓐ Ⓑ	6 0	
58	Ⓐ Ⓒ Ⓑ Ⓓ	6 2 4 0	
59	Ⓑ Ⓐ	6 2	
60	Ⓐ Ⓑ	6 0	

					Total Points	Your Total Score
Page #9 Total:	90			Total (Pages: 8-9)	360	

	GRAND TOTAL POINTS	YOUR GRAND TOTAL SCORE
GRAND TOTAL (Pages 1-9)	1,230	

CALCULATE YOUR CHANCES OF SURVIVING A ZOMBIE OUTBREAK

Your Score	Total Points	Your Grade
	÷ 1,230 =	

Notes:

Notes:

Notes:

Notes:

Notes:

Notes:

ABOUT THE AUTHOR

Casey Bassett is an expert in zombie survival. It is because of his advanced knowledge and skills that he was able to write a detailed test covering the most vital facts to know in the event of a zombie outbreak.

He has studied zombies and survival techniques for the majority of his life, and is dedicated to sharing his knowledge with other zombie survivalists. His goal is to teach and test his fellow survivalists so that they can grow, develop, and strengthen themselves.

Casey believes that the best way of surviving a zombie outbreak is by teaching important survival methods in the event of an attack. *Be proactive, not reactive.* If the human race does not prepare themselves, it will be too late!

ACKNOWLEDGMENTS

Jonathon Burley

Chelsea Bassett

Janelle Farabaugh

Nicole Ferraro

Jake Kornprobst

Zackery Robinson

Thank you all for your time and thoughts! **Remember**... shoot straight.